Practical Guitar Exercises:

Introducing How You Can Supercharge Your Guitar Skills in as Little as 10 Minutes a Day With 75+ Essential Practical Exercises and Tips

By James Haywire

Table of Contents

Introduction

All the guitar schools say the same. For the low price of "huge amount of money" you too can learn to play the guitar! In fact, within just 800 years you'll be a fully-fledged guitar novice!

Not everybody has the time and money to spend so much of it on things like that. Back when I was younger, neither did I. Because of this, I searched for alternative ways to learn. I delved deeper and deeper into how to best optimize my time and spend more of it actually learning.

In this book, I aim to take that to the next level. Turns out, theory is a very small part of the equation when it comes to learning an instrument. In reality, what really matters is practice. You want to do so many exercises that your fingers simply know how to play. Rather than teaching just your brain, you want to get your mind and body in sync.

Now, I've been playing the guitar for a long, long time. Back when I was around 6 or so, my mother enrolled me into a drum lesson class. I actually quite enjoyed the drums. I kept on playing for a few years. I then switched to the flute, which held my attention for even less. I kept on switching from instrument to instrument for years, until one fateful day, I encountered the guitar.

It was back in high school, and a friend of mine had just started playing for the school band. He lent me his guitar so I could have a try, and I was instantly in love. The simplicity of the instrument, and complexity of the sounds dazzled me.

Since then, I've dedicated my life to pursuing the guitar. Today, I've played at some of the most prestigious institutions in the world, and I've led many a musician to the big stage. I spent years and years studying the guitar. But you know, at least half of that time was unnecessary.

Now, you might think I'm speaking gibberish, after all, if it got me so far, how could it be anything but great? Well, you see, while it did get me where I am today, the biggest component of that was my own independent practice. As it turns out, you can't really learn the guitar just by following a teacher.

Most of the theory I've learned in school also never helped me again. While there are some instruments that are honed by theory (such as for example, the piano.) The guitar is an instrument where you'll have more trouble teaching your fingers than you will your brain.

Through all of my years of teaching, not once has a student of mine been hindered by their lack of theoretical knowledge. The way I started to tackle theory was by only referring to it when it was needed. I noticed that the pile of books I had my students read was slowly dwindling until it was just a few short ones.

Now, I'm not saying I can get you playing for the Oxford Orchestra in two days, but I sure as hell can teach you faster than a school can. In this book, I've written down the techniques I teach my students, whom school has failed to teach quickly enough.

If you feel like music school takes too much time, or you don't have enough time to perform 5 hours long playing session just to perfect that one composition you don't even like, then this book is for you.

While this book is designed for those that have little time to commit to their guitar-playing hobby, it was also made with professionalism in mind. This is to say that if you successfully master the techniques presented in this book, you won't be far off becoming a true professional. Can you imagine that? Playing on the big stage, with some of your favorite bands? For most of my students, they are those bands.

Even if all you want to do is play the guitar as a hobby, I guarantee that this book will lay the foundation for your playing in days to come. I don't throw that sentence around willy-nilly, I know full well what material schools and other books will teach you.

If you're truly serious about learning to play the guitar, then this book is the absolute best investment you could possibly make. After all, what's better than learning from a professional?

Note that the tips in this book are quite varied. Some of them are extremely practical, and you'll use them during pretty much every guitar-playing session you'll ever do. The others aren't as practical, but they'll increase the quality of your guitar-playing technique. It's incredible what a set of carefully picked out exercises can really do.

So, you may be wondering, what material does this book cover? Where does it start from?

Well, I will be assuming you have absolutely no guitar knowledge whatsoever. Yes, I do mean none. I'll assume you've heard guitar once or twice on TV, and impulse-bought a random thrift store guitar and you'd like to make it sound as good as possible.

So, if you're an intermediate guitar player, do you get anything from this book? Of course you do. While the book does start itself off on a beginner level, I do pride myself in being able to bring beginners up to speed fairly quickly. Because of this, most of the book will be oriented towards intermediate players.

But what if you're an advanced player? Well, in that case I'd read this book rather selectively. You obviously don't need me to teach you guitar technique, however, what might help you really make it in the guitar playing world is the general tips I'll offer. Keep your eyes out for those and keep on reading!

So, if you're tired of seeing the same tips everywhere, if you're tired of everyone telling you the same things and are looking to try something different, all you've got to do is turn the page!

Chapter 1

Everything You Need to Know About Your Guitar

Do you know your guitar's origin story? While it doesn't strictly help you play better, having an image of how the guitar came to be can come in handy as it'll deepen your connection to the instrument.

Origins of The Guitar

So, the guitar is a plucked, string-based instrument finding its origins in 16th century Spain. The guitar derives its form from the guitarra latina, which was an instrument quite like a modern guitar, except it was narrower, deeper, and had a much less obvious waist.

Even today, Spain hosts some of the most brilliant guitarists in the world and shows off their skills in their flamenco music.

In the beginning, the guitar had 4 courses of strings. Out of these,3 of them were double, while the top one was single. This then ran itself from a pegbox which was much alike to one a violin has, into a bridge that finally connected to the stomach of the instrument.

The initial tuning of the guitar wasn't like today, it was C-F-A-D. If you've studied the lute, then you'll know that these two instruments used to be tuned to the same notes.

The guitar quickly gained popularity from there. As most popular things do, it changed significantly throughout its existence. It didn't even take a hundred years for the fifth course of strings to get added, and not even three hundred before the courses themselves were replaced by single strings. The 1800s were also the time when the standard tuning of today first showed itself: E-A-D-G-B-E. To this day, this tuning has stood the test of time.

The 1600's were a time of evolution for the instrument. Other than the strings, the pegbox itself was also replaced by placing a reflexed head with tuners onto it. The 19th century also brought innovation to this, by substituting the screws that had so far been used to tune the instrument by actual tuning pegs. The frets didn't change as much as the rest, however, the material did change to ivory or metal. Today, there are also plastic ones.

The 19th century marked the time when the guitar's body was the one doing the changing. The guitar became broader, increasing the size of its waist. Further, it became a lot shallower, the soundboard becoming quite thin. On the inside, the reinforcing materials of the guitar were also changed, and the neck got the shape it has today. The changes of the 19th century meddled less with the sound of the guitar, and more with its looks and structural integrity. These innovations were brought to life mostly by Antonio Torres, widely considered the father of the modern-day guitar.

Today, we have various kinds of guitar. Even a basic division like acoustic and electric doesn't really cut it anymore. Today we have 12-stringed guitars, 6-string guitars, bass guitars, and others. The instrument you can see today is a result of hundreds of years of constant refinement.

Initially, guitar notation worked in a system much akin to today's tabs. Over time, the tablature system evolved into its form that we see today, and guitarists began learning traditional sheet music too.

Acoustic Vs Electric Guitar

This is a question that begs itself to be answered to many beginning guitarists. After all, the decision is nowhere near as trivial as it might seem. Deciding to play an acoustic will immediately make you better at certain genres, while an electric guitar is better suited to others.

Unfortunately, this isn't a question I can give you a clear-cut answer, however, I can help you reach your own conclusion.

First of all, if you had a choice, what genre would you want to play? As a beginner, the most important thing is that the type of guitar you pick really connects with you and makes you enjoy it, rather than simply being something that you go back to every now and again. In order to get good at it, you'll have to absolutely love it.

If playing in a rock and roll band is your goal, then an electric guitar might be a better choice. On the other hand, if you grew up listening to flamenco or country, then you might be more acoustic-aligned.

Now, let's look over some of the pros and cons of these two types of guitar, shall we?

Acoustic Guitar

Most beginners start to think that the acoustic guitar is the default starting point for all guitar players. The impression that only upon mastering the acoustic guitar can you play the electric one is extremely far away from the truth. While sure, the acoustic guitar is more commonly found lying around in a household, if you're down to buying a guitar, that shouldn't be of much consequence to you.

It's Cheaper

By this, I don't mean that an acoustic guitar is cheaper than an electric one. After all, there are electric guitars you can get for what amounts to be pocket change, however, the amp isn't free.

The amplifier is a necessary component of playing an electric guitar, which makes it the more expensive choice. Furthermore, you'll also need a few accessories, and electricity. This makes an acoustic guitar significantly cheaper in the long run.

A More Focused Experience

If you're someone that loses focus easily, then an acoustic guitar is probably better for you. Electric guitars feature distortion, pedals, and other elements that can mask your playing. This means that an acoustic guitar excels at making your mistakes more obvious, and your successes more impactful when you know they aren't being carried by extras.

Ease of Carrying

An acoustic guitar is extremely mobile. You can literally just pick it up and take it everywhere, you can even be extra fancy and buy a case (I'm kidding, always buy a case.) If you want to just go to your friend's house and jam, you don't need to pack your whole house up, because your guitar fits into a simple case.

Hey, if you'd like to tour the world as a solo guitarist, would you rather carry a 30kg amp or a 5kg guitar? I think the answer makes itself obvious pretty easily. If instead, you'd like to be a street performer, the advice still stands

Electric Guitar

Okay so, it might look like I'm leaning towards an acoustic guitar for beginners, however, I'm much less partial than that, and would like to point out that there's various advantages that starting out with an electric guitar presents.

Ease of Playing

Okay, this will seem like I'm looking down on electric guitar players, however, they are quite a bit easier to play than their acoustic cousins, at least on a beginner level.

Acoustic guitars are generally quite a bit more difficult to start out with. This is due to their higher action (the strings are positioned further away from the fretboard.) This means that it's much easier to create accurate finger shapes on an electric guitar. As a beginner, you won't have much flexibility, or strength in your fingers. This can make it a lot more difficult to start out on an acoustic than an electric guitar.

You Can Control the Volume Better

Okay so, when most people think of an electric guitar, they think of a rock-and-roll monstrosity that can absolutely get your blood pumping. Well, this is one way of playing an electric guitar. However, what most people don't know, is that the knob on your average amp goes both ways. Yes, this means you can actually play at a much lower noise level than an acoustic guitar. This means that in case your landlord, parents, or partner aren't fond of the noise you're making, you can practice with low volume! In case you need to stay absolutely silent, there's no question about electric being the superior choice, as you can even plug your headphones into it!

More Effects & Variety

The electric guitar allows you to access a wide array of different sounds that it can make. It also allows you to distort the sound that you're making. This makes it intrinsically more flexible than the acoustic guitar. Furthermore, the electric guitar is way easier to tune how you like it than an acoustic guitar is.

This comparison should've helped you decide between the electric and acoustic guitar. Don't worry too much though, as regardless of what you choose, you'll be able to learn to play just fine. It doesn't take a Van Hallen to play the electric guitar, nor does it take an Estas Tonne to make a good sound on an acoustic.

A crucial part of learning how to play the guitar is precisely this, you need to set your aims. If you're planning to go big as a Rockstar, then don't pick the acoustic guitar, if you're planning to play flamenco outside on the street daily, then don't go for the electric.

How Does A Guitar Make Sound?

Looking at a guitar get played can be quite mystifying, how does it make that pleasant sound just by having strings pulled? Today, I'm here to explain that to you.

Acoustic

As you might've guessed, the acoustic and electric guitars make their sounds in different ways. The guitar makes its sound much in the same way that all other string-based instruments do. The strings being struck/plucked makes them vibrate on a given frequency.

The length of the string, as well as its weight and tension, will determine the frequency at which this vibration happens. The shorter a string is, the higher the frequency, the heavier a string is, the lower the frequency. Naturally, the tenser a string is, it will also produce a higher-sounding frequency.

This is why the thickest strings on the guitar make the deepest noise, they're heavier than the rest. The length of the strings affecting the sound becomes apparent when you think about the fretting process. The guitarist puts their fingers on the fret, essentially shortening the string for a short amount of time.

A more advanced technique is to push the string across the fret. This makes the string stretch ever so slightly and gives an interesting effect to the music.

Surprisingly enough, the electric guitar doesn't work all that differently. While it isn't the same, it is quite similar. The electric guitar uses the strings, supported by the magnets under the strings (called pickups.) These then make an electric current that will change up the pickup's magnetic field. In turn, this field will start to oscillate at the same frequency as the string you just pulled.

Then, this current is transferred through the guitar. The wires carry the frequency encoded in them via wires until they reach the amp. At this point, the amp will take more power from its power supply, intensifying the current. The current itself, while being more powerful, stays on the same frequency as when it started. This then travels to a big magnet that alters its position to a cone. The cone then begins to push out air. This then makes the characteristic noise that we associate with an electric guitar.

Strings & Frets on A Guitar

If you'd like to get a bunch of guitarists in a room to start fighting (I'm not judging you.) All you have to do is ask them how many strings and frets a guitar should have. You've just created a bloodbath.

There's a variety of different kinds of guitar, and every guitarist will swear by it that theirs is the ideal one. In reality, there is no perfect number of frets, no perfect number of strings. If there were, we'd all be playing the same guitar, and I think the musical variety the instrument brings is a blessing, rather than something to fight over.

Pretty much every guitar has frets. Frets are metal strips that are attached to the fretboard on points that will provide a certain frequency. All this is calculated according to some fairly complex mathematical formulae.

There are, however, fretless guitars. These are usually bass guitars, however, rarely there does come along an actually fretless guitar.

Most classical guitars will have 19 frets. Their electric cousins composing between 21 and 24 instead. With that being said, some compositions require even more frets than this, resulting in guitars that can sometimes have a whopping 27 frets.

If you've played the piano or another instrument, then you'll know the concept of an octave. It's 8 consecutive root notes, and on the guitar that is laid out over 12 frets. This means that frets are made for every half-step.

The number of strings is equally varied. Chances are, you've never seen a guitar with any less or more than 6 strings. With that being said, they do exist.
Firstly, there are 12-strings monsters that feature 6 double-stringed courses. These tend to be a lot more difficult to play, though they do give a unique sound.

In metal music, you'll often find that the lead guitarist is using a 7 or 8 string guitar. These guitars are made to have extra bass strings, making it easier to reach the lower tones. 7-8 string guitars are also fairly common in the complex rhythms of jazz music and lay the ground for certain basslines.

20's and 30's music was famous for its 4-string guitars. These are called tenor guitars, and while they were largely out of use for most of their existence, they're currently having a bit of a revival.

If that wasn't enough, there are also 9-string guitars. These work much like their 12-string counterparts, except they leave the bass strings as single.

That's not even the end, "harp" guitars also exist. These will often have more than 10, and sometimes even over 15 strings. With that being said, on these you only play 6, leaving the rest just to resonate with those.

So, what you should be getting from this is that the number of frets and strings on a guitar is extremely variable. Depending on what it is used for, the guitar's components are freely changed. With that being said, this book was designed to help you with learning a 6-string, 19-fret guitar. This can easily be extended to a 24-fret guitar, however, if your guitar is fretless, you might face some issues.

Tuning Your Guitar

There is a variety of different ways you can tune your guitar. All of them essentially boil down to manipulating the tuners on the head of the guitar in order to make the pitch of a string align with how it "should" sound.

In this small tutorial, we'll be looking over how to tune your guitar according to the standard tuning. As a beginner, the standard tuning is all you'll need.

First of all, you need to know how the strings are numbered. They're numbered with numbers from 1 to 6 starting with the highest. In ascending order, starting with the sixth string, the strings of the guitar are E, A, D, G, B, and E. The reason both the first and last strings are named "E" is that they're exactly one octave apart in pitch.

Tuning Your Guitar Using A Pitch Tuner

Tuning your guitar with a chromatic or a pitch tuner is definitely the easiest way to accomplish it. It's extremely important that you have a method that reliably tells you if you're tuning right or wrong. Usually, a guitarist will use either an app or a different instrument in order to tune their guitar.

As a beginner, an app will do just fine. Alternatively, you can use a tuner. For example, a chromatic tuner hears the note you're playing, and tells you the pitch at which it's currently. This lets you be able to tell if the note you're playing is too high or low.

Pitch tuners are a lot harder to use. They will play a perfect pitch for each string, and you'll be forced to match the sound by ear.

My personal recommendation is to just use a tuning app. These make the tuning process a lot easier, and analog tools can only get you so far before you get frustrated with them. Sure, if you've got perfect tone hearing then a pitch tuner might be great, but an app will still be faster.

You can also use a tuning fork, which you just strike in order to have it make the right pitch for the string.

If you're a visual learner, then using a chromatic tuner is a good idea, as it'll let you know whether you're doing it right or wrong right off the bat rather than letting you make mistakes.

If you've got an ear for these things, you might use a pitch tuner or the fork.

14

On the other hand, if you'd just like to get on with it and tune your guitar, just download a tuning app on your phone or computer and be done with it.

Tuning the Guitar Without Use of A Pitch Tuner

Now, let's say your phone battery is dead, there isn't an electronic device within reach, but you absolutely must tune your guitar for the most crucial challenge of your life, then what do you do?

Well, what you do is tune your other strings to one you think is most tuned. First, you'll begin by adjusting your 6th string. Place your finger on its 5th fret, this is the A note on the E string. Now, play the 5th string until the sounds match, you've successfully tuned the 5th string to the 6th. It can also be rather useful to know how to hum the right note, as it'll help you hear better whether or not your string is too tightly tuned, or if it's too loose instead.

Afterward, you'll want to tune the D string so that it matches the pitch of your A string when you put your finger on its 5th fret and play. You can continue this trend down the neck of your guitar for every string except B. When it comes to tuning the B string properly, you'll need to hold the G string on its 4th fret instead.

If you're playing a solo, this will make your guitar sound fine, this is because even if it's not tuned to any specific tuning, it's still tuned to itself.

How To Tune A Guitar Using A Keyboard

So, let's say you don't have a tuner at hand, but you've got a piano or keyboard for some God forsaken reason. You can still get your guitar in tune with the piano without much of an issue. Tuning to a keyboard is a perfect way to tune your guitar in case you're playing with another instrument. It's standard for every member of an orchestra or band to be tuned to the same piano, rather than a theoretical tuning.

The only thing you need to do is tune the 6th string so that it's the same note as the one two octaves below the middle C. Then you just reiterate what we've just learned.

Exercises:

1. Hand your guitar to someone that hasn't played in their lifetime. Let them get the guitar completely out of tune, then try using an app to tune the guitar back properly.
2. Get your guitar out of tune (you can use an app to make sure every string is out of tune.) Try to do this by different amounts, and then leave the app and tune the guitar to itself. That'll help you play in conditions where you don't have a tuner
3.(Bonus exercise) Research other tunings online, try to determine how you could tune your guitar to those, check against the app!

Chapter 2

For the Complete Noob

If you're just starting out with the guitar, the first thing you'll need to learn is how to read the different kinds of notational systems guitarists have made to make playing easier.

While learning and playing by ear might be interesting, you can't learn everything by ear (or at least 99.99% of guitarists can't.) Because of this, we have systems in place to make reading music easier. Sheet music is by far the hardest to learn on the guitar, while chord diagrams are the easiest.

Chord Diagrams

Reading a chord diagram is one of the most important parts of learning the guitar. These are small, bite-sized chunks of learning that will teach you a specific chord (a combination of notes making a pleasant sound.) By the time you're done with this chapter, reading chord diagrams will have become as easy as reading this sentence.

Let's take a look at the chord diagram below:

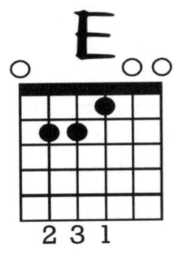

This is the E-major chord, and it's one of the most commonly used guitar chords out there.

So, let's start off from the top. The black bar that you see at the very top of the chord diagram represents the nut. The nut is the part at the very end of the fretboard, which helps the strings and fretboard stick close.

Then, every row underneath that represents a different one of the frets. The first row is the 1st fret, while the 2nd is the 2nd fret, this continues on and on forever (though realistically you'll rarely see anything separated by more than 2-3 frets on the same chord diagram.)

As you've noticed, there aren't only horizontal lines on that diagram, there are also vertical ones. The vertical lines are a representation of the 6 guitar strings. They go from right to left. Meaning the rightmost line represents the E string, the thinnest string on the guitar. It's the one that's found closest to your head and the line which goes all the way to the left is the 6th, thickest string.

The numbers underneath the diagram are crucial for understanding it, they are telling you which fingers to use at which strings. These are the fingers of your non-dominant, fretting hand. In case you see T instead of a number, then that means that you should use your thumb instead of your other 4 fingers.

But, I hear you ask, what are the dots for then? The black dots which you see on every chord diagram are telling you which fret you should be pressing down on. Sometimes, you'll also see some circles above the nut of the guitar, this means that you shouldn't be fretting those strings at all.

So, looking back on the E major diagram, just put your middle finger on the 2nd fret of the A string, then put your ring finger on the 2nd fret of the D string. Your index finger should go on the 1st fret of the G string. For the strings that have empty circles (E, B, E) you'll play them but won't fret them.

In case you see an "X" instead of a circle above the nut, then that means that string isn't played at all in the chord you're trying to play.

You might also see a curved line above the nut of your guitar on the chord diagram. This means that you use the same finger to fret multiple strings. These chords are referred to as the "barre" chords.

Now, you might be curious, aren't there any chords above the 5th fret? If you are indeed curious, then you'll be happy to find out that there indeed are chords past the 5th fret. These are written down next to the diagram, for example, the Eb minor chord starts from the 6th fret. Because of that, it'll have a "6fr" written down next to it, in order to signalize that the chord begins on the 6th fret.

You might also see just a 6 or VI instead of this, but just know that the number to the right of the chord diagram means it starts from a fret past the first 5.

Exercises:

1. Try making your own chord diagram! Once you've learned a chord, try drawing it out on a chord diagram. That'll help you learn which notes are in the chord, and how they're played.
2. Take a look at the figure below, try reading the chords:

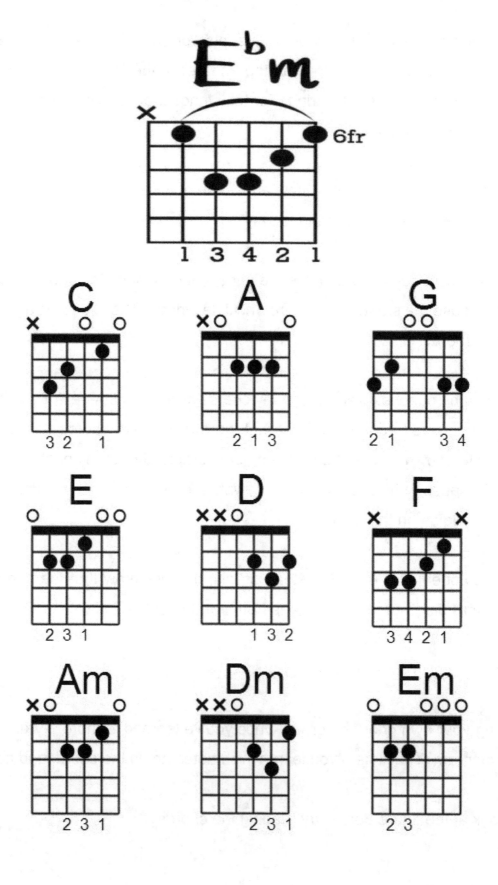

20

3. Which of the chords above are:

A) Barre?

B) Start after the 5th fret?

C) Have open strings?

Rhythm Slashes

Rhythm slashes are much less commonly used than chord diagrams, however, that's not to say they're way less useful. Their purpose mainly lies in the fact that they can easily help you learn songs. Not all songs are full of fingerpicking, some songs you simply need to know the chords and the durations.

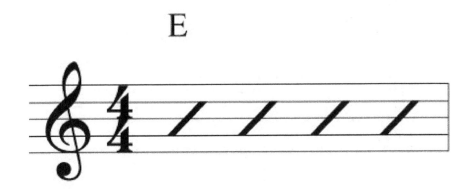

Pictured above is one measure of the E chord. The chord symbol is above the staff (the set of lines and spaces.) The 4 notches just mean "play an E chord 4 times."

Exercises:

1. Try playing the rhythm slashes above, refer to the chord diagrams in the section before this one.

Guitar Tablature

Guitar tablature is quite similar to chord diagrams, except turned horizontally. Guitar tabs are by far the most common way of writing down guitar music. While you will see some standard notation on the top and bottom of the tab, they're usually void of this.

The six strings of your guitar are appropriately described by the 6 horizontal lines present on a tab. The high E string is represented by the bottom line on the tab (this is the 6th string.) While this is a bit counterintuitive, you can just keep in mind that tabs are essentially inverted. The top string is thinnest, and the bottom string is thickest.

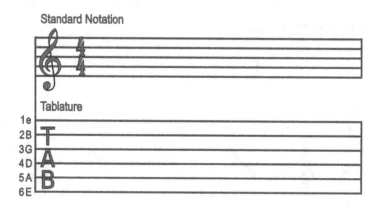

Tabs are always read from the left to the right. You'll only play two notes at the same time in case they're written on top of each other. Otherwise, you'll play them one after the other in a given manner.

The notes on tablature aren't represented by shapes, unlike sheet music. Instead, they're represented by numbers. These numbers dictate where you should be putting your fingers. These are also read left to right, much like a book.

Chords, on the other hand, are written one on top of the other instead. When you see stacked numbers, you'll know it's a chord. If the finger you're seeing is "0" that means you leave the string open and don't touch it.

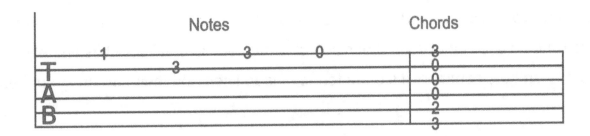

Exercises:

1. Start reading tabs! Go to a site like https://www.ultimate-guitar.com/ and start reading tabs today. For example, check out Knockin' On Heaven's Door.

2. Write down a tab! Try listening to a simple piece of music (for example, Twinkle Twinkle Little Star.) And keep writing down tabs until you've got the melody right.

Muting

Okay so, we've gone over the most crucial element of reading guitar tabs, however, there are still some more advanced guitar techniques you should know the notation of. One of them is muting. Muting is the practice of controlling a note's duration by slowly lowering its pitch until its silent.

Palm muting is represented by a "P.M.-" marker on a guitar tab, and the little dashes are representing for how long you should keep palm muting the notes. To palm mute a note means to put the side of your hand slightly underneath the little finger across all the strings you need to pluck. Then you pluck while consistently dampening their sound. While it is called palm muting, it's a bit of a misnomer, as you do it with the side of your hand.

This is also referred to as pizzicato in professional music. This is due to the fact that it makes the guitar sound much like a bowed string instrument.

Muted notes, also called dead notes, are denoted with a small X on a string. This means that you should use one of your hands and play the note so that its pitch is entirely muted. While this isn't too common, it's often found in lead lines and their strumming patterns.

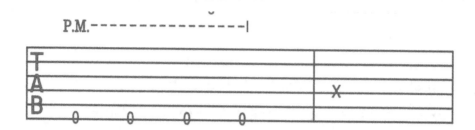

Exercises:

1. Try muting! Play one of the tabs above and try muting a note or two.

2. Use palm muting when playing chords, try playing different chords and muting various notes, how does that affect the sound?

3. Bonus exercise: These are only some of the musical elements that can be represented on a tab, find out online what the rest are!

Sheet Music

Despite many guitarist's insistence that they "don't need sheet music because they have tabs" sheet music has remained the king of music notation, even in the guitar. But why do we need sheets? After all, wouldn't it be possible for us to play every single composition ever just by using tabs?

Actually, yes it would. Unfortunately, not every composition ever has been written down in tabs and denoting certain parts of music with tablature isn't very practical.

So, you should be learning sheet music so that you can feel confident in your ability to play any given piece of music.

Symbols and Notation

Music is made by using a variety of different symbols, the most essential ones being the staff, clefs, and individual notes. Every piece of music will have all three of these, it will be written in a staff, contain notes, and will have clefs. To read sheet music, you'll need to know all of these.

The staff is made of five lines and four spaces in between each of those. Every line and space represents a different letter from A to G. This means that the 8 notes that exist are "A, B, C, D, E, F, and G." These notes can also be said in a different way, it being "Do, Re, Mi, Fa, Sol, La, Si." You'll find that these notes move up the staff in alphabetical order of progression.

THE STAFF

The Clefs are the first thing you'll see when you take a gander at a piece of sheet music. They look like ornate, calligraphic letters, and that's basically what they are. When it comes to music that you'll be playing on the guitar, you'll only need the treble clef, looking like a fancier G. This clef is used to describe higher frequencies and more high-pitched notes. It's often used for violin and flute as well.

Now, you might be facing some trouble remembering the notes on the treble clef at first, for this, there are a few word games that'll make it incredibly easy. Let's take, for example the sentence "Every Good Boy Does Fine." If we take the first letter from every word, then we'll get the notes on the lines in treble clef "E, G, B, D, and F."

When it comes to the notes found in spaces, then you should simply remember the word "Face." This is because the notes that lie in the spaces of the treble clef are "F, A, C, and E"

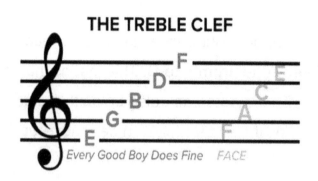

Every Good Boy Does Fine   FACE

Exercises:

1. Open up any composition in treble clef, it can be something as simple as Twinkle Twinkle Little Star. Just read the notes in it out loud, one by one.

2. Try going for a more complex piece now, for example, Led Zeppelin's Stairway To Heaven.

Musical Notes

So, one thing we've learned so far is that depending on where a note is on the staff, it tells you how you should play it on the guitar. Notes also tell you how long you should play them, they're made out of three components:

1. The Note Head- The note head is possessed by every note and can be filled or empty. It's the circular part of the note, and we identify notes by where their head ends up.

2. The Note Stem- The note stem is the "neck" of the note and will be found pointing either up or down depending on the note's location.

3. The Note Flag- The flag is used to indicate a note's duration and looks like a "wing" on the note stem.

If you've ever played another instrument, you'll know that it's possible to add ledger lines underneath the staff to gain "extra" notes you can play with.
Now then, let's take a look at the different values notes can hold.

NOTE VALUES

NOTE VALUES

The largest note is the whole note, and its duration is 4 beats. It's the simplest of all notes to write, being made up of only an empty note head. The whole note doesn't possess a stem nor a flag. The closest thing to it is the half note, which naturally lasts for half as long as a whole note, 2 beats. It doesn't have a filled note head, but it does have a note stem.

A quarter note then lasts for 1 beat or a quarter of a whole note. It has a note stem, as well as being the first note to have a filled note head.

Smaller than the quarter note is the eighth note. It's made up of a filled note head, note stem, as well as a note flag. It lasts for only half a beat and is the second smallest of the notes we'll be looking at here.

The sixteenth note lasts for half an eighth or a total of 1/16 of a whole note. It has a filled note head, note stem, and two note flags.

There are more ways to establish a duration for a given note other than just writing it down as a different one. For example, we could put a dot next to the note's head. This means that we should add 0.5 of the note to its duration. For example, a quarter note would last 1.5 beats, while an eighth would last one-sixth of a beat.

Another way is legato, which is denoted by a curved line connecting two different notes. Legato means that you should hold the note under the curved line for as long as the curved line goes.

Exercises:

1. How much does a whole note with a dot next to it last?
2. Which is longer, three eighth notes with a dot, or a quarter note?

BEAMING

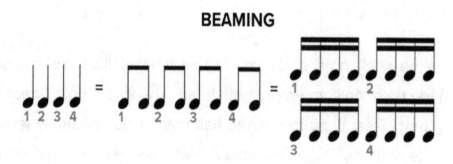

Beaming is a technique that simplifies the writing of eighth and sixteenth notes. Instead of writing down the note flag, if there are 2 eighth or sixteenth notes next to each other, we can just add a horizontal line connecting the two.

In case when you don't want a note somewhere, you can use a rest. Rests are often used to help the musician regain composure, after all, strumming away at the guitar for 3 hours without rest would be nigh-impossible.

Much like notes, rests have durations too.

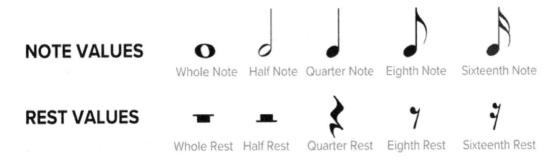

Exercises:

1. Pick a composition and beat-read it, I would advise using Back In Black by AC/DC as an example. By beat-read, I mean you should read every note as if it just had a rhythmic value. Have one beat be represented by say, a single clap of hands.

2. This is a bit more difficult but try using the song below and reading it with notes too. Whenever you see a note, read its rhythmic value together with clapping for the appropriate number of beats.

ENA (Bassline)

As recorded by Haustor

Transcribed by L'gavrue

A Verse

♩ = 105

Gtr I

B Chorus

This is a bit difficult, so don't get flustered if it's not completely clear to you at first. If you're struggling with it too much, then give it another shot, this time doubling the note durations.

Beats

We've already talked about note durations in terms of "beats", but we've never defined a beat, have we? Well, turns out that a "beat" is something much like time, you know what it is, but it's tough to define. According to music theory, a beat is the most basic unit of rhythm and dictates the flow of the song.

To play a song, you'll need to know the piece's meter. The meter is a way of saying how many beats there are in a single measure in the song. The meter is found straight after the clef and is written down with a fraction.

The topmost number will notify you of the number of beats we have in a measure. The bottom number is there to tell you how much every beat's value is. Generally, you'll find that this number is 4, meaning that a quarter lasts for 1 beat.

To take an example, let's take a look at Twinkle Twinkle Little Star. The time signature within this song is 4/4. This means that a measure within it contains 4 beats, and every quarter note is valued at just a single beat.

On the other hand, some songs have different signatures. For example, Over The River And Through The Woods has a time signature of ¾. This means that every measure contains 3 beats, and a quarter still lasts 4 beats.

Exercise: Listen to both of these songs while counting the beats. When it comes to Twinkle Twinkle Little Star, you'll want to count "One Two Three Four." For Over The River And Through The Woods, you should be counting "one two three."

A mistake beginners often make is confusing a beat with a note. You could have 98 notes within a 4/4 measure and not be off in the slightest. In the same vein, you could have a lone whole note occupy the same space. A half note with a dot and two eighths does the same thing.

The final part of rhythm we need to learn about is tempo. The tempo is written down in BPM or beats per minute. For example, a 60BPM tempo would mean that you're playing 60 quarter note equivalents every minute.

Chapter 3

Start with Daily Good Habits

Learning anything in this world isn't easy, and this isn't limited to just the guitar. In this chapter, we'll be exploring the importance of continuity in guitar practice.

The guitar, like most instruments, is fundamentally something you learn to play through your fingers, rather than your head. You might know exactly how, and where to play every single note, but if your fingers aren't capable of following that line of thought, well, then you aren't playing the guitar are you?

Unfortunately, while your brain might remember everything just from reading it once, your fingers won't.

Instruments are learned through muscle memory, and you won't be building that by simply playing for 4 hours every week. You need to make sure that you practice in relatively short intervals, as longer intervals between practice sessions make it a lot more difficult to get back into the groove later.

Because of this, it's a lot more effective to simply play the guitar for say, 5 minutes every day than 2 hours every week. This is in spite of the 2nd amount being almost twice as long as the first.

Posture

This is one of the most common things for beginners to struggle with. Most beginner guitarists aren't familiar with the importance of posture in playing this instrument.

Even some intermediate guitarists have problems with this. Professionals, well, it happens, but those usually don't last very long due to a combination of back and wrist issues.

Posture is arguably the most important thing there is to playing the guitar. Sure, actually playing it is nice but is it really worth it if you're sacrificing your health at an alarming rate?

It's important to know how to play both sitting down and standing up, because of that, I'll be teaching you how to hold your guitar in both positions. Don't forget that audiences get hyped up when the guitarist stands up, use that to your advantage.

Posture When Sitting

Usually, you'll want to sit in a place that has some degree of back support, such as next to a wall, or on a chair. Now, put the waist of the guitar on your dominant side's leg. You should be holding the back of the guitar supported by your belly and torso. The neck of the guitar should be parallel to the floor.

A mistake commonly made here is using the non-dominant hand to support the neck from falling downwards to the floor. Rather than do this, let your dominant arm sit on the top of the guitar's body. Feel free to adjust your position until everything feels comfortable.

Now, your non-dominant (fretting) hand should have its thumb be behind the neck of the guitar. It should find itself more or less lying in between your first two fingers.

When fretting, make sure that you're using your fingertips only, you don't want to be putting your whole finger on the fretboard. In the same vein, make sure to keep your nails trimmed, as putting them on the fretboard doesn't produce the best sound in the world.

To position your dominant (strumming) hand, first, you'll want to put your upper arm on the top part of the body of the guitar. Your dominant hand should be hovering over the sound hole of the guitar. Make sure not to tense up your hand while doing this, as this can lead to wrist issues.

Posture when standing up is pretty much the same, except you use your non-dominant hand to hold the guitar up, while a strap that goes around your neck supports its alignment.

Strumming Properly

Strumming properly is crucial to maintaining your health while playing the guitar. The most commonly used strumming technique is:

1. Put your thumb next to your 1st finger and keep them like that.
2. Bend the rest of your fingers towards the middle of your hand.
3. Start strumming, use your index finger's nail in order to strum the string, and when you're strumming upwards, use the nail of your thumb.

You can enhance the sound of this by growing out your nails on these fingers. Furthermore, the same technique can be done with your middle finger, however, you'll need to pay extra attention that your index finger doesn't get in the way.

Basic Injury Prevention

There are a few crucial steps to preventing guitar-related injuries.

1. Keep your back straight- not doing this is similar to sitting in a chair for a prolonged period of time while slouched. It can cause back issues in the future, as well as a bent neck.

2. Make sure that your neck and shoulders are relaxed- having a stiff neck can cause injury to it when moved. The shoulders can get injured, and also get in the way of your playing.

3. Get rid of any tension present in your arms- finger and wrist tension can leave you with lifelong injuries if left unchecked, so always make sure that you're as relaxed as possible before playing.

4. Stretch- even professional guitarists will sometimes take a break on stage. Make sure you aren't overexerting yourself while playing.

5. Stay healthy- no matter how good your posture while playing is, if you aren't staying healthy in general, your health isn't going to be in the best state ever.

Warming Up & Exercising

Before playing, it's extremely important to warm up, this whole section will be made up of different guitar exercises to make blood start flowing through your fingers.

Exercises:

1. A great way to start off guitar practice is by getting your circulation going and making your hands and fingers loose and unrestrained. The first requirement for this is heat.

Have you ever tried playing the guitar with cold hands? Let me tell you, it isn't the most pleasant of experiences.

2. So, get a faucet and crank that hot water up. Now, I'm not saying scorch your skin off the face of the earth, but make sure that it's enough to warm you up well. While the water is going over your hands, you'll want to extend your fingers as much as you can. Stretch them and loosen them repeatedly until the cold goes away from your hands.

Now, before your hands start feeling dry, you'll want to get them sweating a bit with some of my warm-up exercises.

The next few exercises are there to get your fretting hand ready to play, as well as to loosen up your picking hand. There are a few rules for the exercises I'm about to tell you:

Always begin slowly, many beginner-level guitarists start out trying to play the piece as quickly as possible. This isn't good for learning music, nor for exercising. The most important thing is that you're playing the piece correctly, the speed can be improved upon later.

Take note that some of the exercises I'm about to show you utilize alternate picking, so don't try to get sloppy! While you could play these without using alternate picking, that's not what they were designed for.

2. Play a few scales. Playing scales will develop your fingerpicking skills greatly. If you aren't familiar with the way scales are played, let me explain. You start at a given note, then fingerpick the first 8 tones of it, then you reverse direction and play that way. For example, let's give the below scale a shot:

I think you've got the idea, basically, go over them forward and backward. If you're having trouble with which scales to go over, don't worry, you can check out some online.

3. Chords. Chords are a guitarist's bread and butter, and you'll need to know a wide variety if you're planning to become a successful guitarist. The thing there is that you want to focus on alternating chords, as well as playing them with alternating picking. What this means is that you don't want to stick with the same chord for more than 1-2 strums (unless you're practicing strumming.) And instead want to mix them up. Play one, then switch to the other. At first, doing this with two chords will be enough, but you'll find that as you add more and more, you'll get a lot better at playing, and especially fretting.

4. Play the finger dexterity exercise below. I'll admit, it looks pretty intimidating, but with a little practice, you'll get the hang of it. It is made to test out how dexterous the fingers on your fretting hand are, so are you up to the task?

5. Freestyle! Try mixing up the last three exercises and make some of your own styles. A common mistake beginners make is that they just follow the protocol down to a T. Rather than doing this, you should instead opt to jam as much as possible because it is what really tests your playing skills. Jamming shows your skills at playing the instrument itself, rather than just your ability to play someone else's music. This is why most famous guitarists always have a jamming session before they start filming.

6. Let's go back down to Earth now. The last three exercises are there to help your brain and fingers get on the same page, but they're a bit too stressful to be done whenever you'd like, so I've got an easy one for you now. All you have to do is play the first, second, third, and fourth fret on every string.

Sounds simple enough right? Well, it is, and it'll help relax your fingers, as the exercises above can tense up a beginner due to being a tad challenging. This one is also quick to do, and you can check how fast you're able to do it as a measure of your progress.

7. Sometimes when you don't have a guitar, you can still get some practice in. Playing chords, or even individual strings on an "air guitar" is better practice than no practice. Maybe you're waiting for your turn at the doctor's, sitting in the car's backseat, or are in one of the millions of different situations where you won't have a guitar available, you can simply imagine one and play away. I'm not going to tell you this practice is better than having a guitar, but it's sure as hell better than having none.

Chapter 4

Wisely Use Your 5 Minutes Everyday

In this chapter, we'll be looking at how to properly min-max your time using the Pareto principle and other tricks. I swear, it isn't as intimidating as it sounds. Essentially, this chapter is for the 21st working person that has to work 8 hours a day and be available for "online meetings" for another 3. Obviously you won't get much time for the guitar, but even the little time you have can bring you up another level as long as you use it wisely.

The Pareto Principle

You've probably heard of the Pareto or 80/20 principle. Whether it being your friend complaining that 80% of women go for 20% of men, or a computer scientist saying how 20% of bugs generally cause 80% of crashes out there.

Even if you've heard of it, you might not have completely understood it. For one, it doesn't have to be 20 and 80, or 10 and 90 or any pair of numbers that adds up to 100.

For example, you could have 10% of workers doing 50% of the result. Or it could be 40% or 99%, it doesn't matter. The basic principle behind the Pareto principle is that a small amount of something can cause a much greater amount of change.

It's useful because it lends itself to the idea that a minority of inputs could contribute to the majority of outcomes. So, what does this mean in guitar terms?

Well, it basically means that in 20-30 minutes of practice, you could achieve 80% of the improvement of someone practicing for 2-3 hours. Practice, like most things, gives diminishing returns.

As we all know, concentration diminishes over time. While you might be up and alert during the first 10 minutes of playing, can you say the same about the piece you're playing 3 hours from then?

The Pareto principle lets you take a small amount of time, say 5 minutes, and shows us that more work gets done then than the next 2 hours, comparatively speaking at least.

Sure, some of us need some time to get into the groove, but that isn't important. The most important thing it shows is that you can practice for a short amount of time and still get great results!

So, how do you incorporate this principle into learning if you've got a bunch of time to learn? Are you just doomed to practice for 2 hours and only get 20% more returns than if you'd done it for 30 minutes?

Fortunately, that isn't the case either, and you can still make the Pareto principle work for you. Let's say that at first, you spent 30 minutes practicing with chords. Now, you're planning on continuing your practice for another 1:30 hours. But why would you do that for just 20% of the returns?

The solution is to switch away from chords. Start practicing, say, scales. The change of material will spark a bit of excitement in you, helping you stay alert and concentrate on the new material. Now, you can spend another 30 minutes practicing that, and then move on to say, that song you've always wanted to learn.

Now, this doesn't completely delete diminishing returns, you'll still slowly get more and more tired, and less and less information will get memorized by your brain and fingers. Despite this, you'll make a lot more progress than if you'd just kept on practicing chords for the full two hours.

Parkinson's Law

Surprisingly enough, learning the guitar is infested with a wide variety of business laws and principles. Parkinson's law is one such example.

It's a law descending from the world of business and states "work expands so as to fill the time available for its completion." Or in other words "people will do something in as much time as you give them." While this is generally used in order to justify shorter deadlines for things in the workplace, it works especially well when it comes to self-study.

Have you noticed that when you decide you'll do something on a given day, you always somehow finish close to the evening? On the other hand, even when you say you'll do the same thing in 2 hours, it's done in 2 hours?

This is because of Parkinson's law, the more time you have, the more you feel like you don't need to work quickly, and can take tiny breaks in between. In reality, you're able to do it much faster, but since you have the luxury of more time, it's taking you more time to do it.

Because of this, you shouldn't have overly long practice sessions. In fact, it's better to have them be too short than too long. In a session that's too long, you might just wind up not getting around to doing what you wanted. In one that's too short, you're cramming every second of time with something useful, and this is making you much faster at it.

Only give yourself as much time as you *need*, the moment you have an excess of time, you'll take a snack, a long break etc. and potentially wind up not completing the task.

Try to set milestones for your practice sessions. For example, "I'll learn to play this song in the next hour." Then, if you don't manage to do it in an hour, just keep trying until you're able to. On the other hand, if you've managed it within an hour, you've done something that would've probably taken you 2-3 hours if you gave yourself that time.

Sometimes, shorter sessions like this can provide greater results, especially when combined with the Pareto principle. Furthermore, by setting multiple small milestones, you're avoiding the pitfalls of both Parkinson's law and the Pareto principle.

The #1 Ingredient to Guitar Success

People often ask me, what's the secret of the musicians on the big stage? What is it they have that they don't? How can some people improve so quickly while others are stuck in mediocrity for a while?

Now, there are obviously a lot of factors going into this. Talent, luck, social background, and many other circumstances go into it, but I can tell you the biggest thing that separates a mediocre guitarist from a great one is none of those things.

"Then what is it?" I hear you ask. The Pareto principle? Using Parkinson's law to their advantage? In reality, it's none of those. The element that is most responsible for the difference between say, you and Slash, is habit.

Habit is the core of all guitar-playing skills. In fact, habit is an essential portion that makes learning anything easier.

Studies have shown that simply making something a habit, which is to say, a crucial part of your daily routine can go a long way in helping you learn it.

So, how exactly do you form a habit?

First of all, you'll have to do it at the same time every day. Would you get into the habit of going to school if school was at a different hour every day? In that same way, you should try to space out your playing sessions so that they occur at roughly the same time/s every day.

By doing this, it'll be much easier to push through that "rut" feeling. It's that feeling that you get when you don't know what to do with yourself, but you know that you sure as hell won't do whatever you're supposed to. Procrastination is the biggest enemy of habit, and by playing at the same time every day, you'll be getting yourself used to pushing past it.

Never make excuses. The moment you make an excuse the first time, and miss out on playing, is when you'll cascade into making more. Learning the guitar is similar to going to the gym. Sure, the end result is great, but are you ready to endure the drive until you get to the end result? In order to do this, you need to be a bit cold to yourself. Let's say you've got a cold, under those conditions you shouldn't play the guitar, right? No.

Even if you might not learn much due to your brain being clouded by illness, the important thing is that you're keeping up the habit.

Another important thing to remember is that it's much easier to change a habit than to make one anew. So, if you're planning on making your playing sessions longer, don't just decide you'll have them at a different portion of the day, try to make it so that you're having them at around the same time.

Exercises:

1. Remind yourself of the Pareto principle, think about how it can be used for learning the guitar, as well as your daily life.

2. Make a small habit, I challenge you to play the guitar at 9:55 PM for 5 minutes, anywhere you'd like. Can you keep this up for a month?

3. Try meditating. Sure, it isn't exactly a guitar technique, but it has been shown to make creating habits easier.

Chapter 5
Left Hand Techniques

When we say "left hand" in guitar-playing, what we mean is your non-dominant hand. There are guitarists out there that switch this around, fretting with their right and playing with their lefts.

Regardless of whether you're just starting out in guitar, or if you've been playing for years, it's never too late to get the basics down. Oftentimes when more veteran guitarists came to me for help, their issues boiled down to fundamentals.

While making sure your left-hand technique is flawless might seem simple, it's far from it, and the payoffs you'll be getting from learning it are massive. Arguably, it's even more important than right-hand technique.

Correct Positioning

Positioning your left hand the right way is crucial not only to playing effectively but also to making sure you stay without injury. So, without further ado, let's see the 4 principles of left-hand positioning:

1. Make Sure It's Loose and Relaxed- While this sounds a bit strange, obvious even, it can give trouble to even professional guitarists. Oftentimes, you'll tense up when anticipating a hard part of a song, and that'll make your left hand tense. By relaxing your muscles, you ensure that the music is able to flow slowly, and you aren't gatekeeping your own playing speed.

Exercise: Try strumming in the air for a few minutes, does your hand hurt? If yes, try running it under hot water and listening to some relaxing music until you can do it properly.

2. Put Your Thumb Where It Should Be- Do not, I repeat, do not put your thumb squarely in the middle of the guitar's neck. I hear this advice repeated ad nauseam, and while it's sometimes useful, generally, you want to rest your thumb closer to the lower strings than the upper ones.

It's also worth making sure that your thumb isn't fixed in one place. While as a beginner, holding your thumb in one location might be enough, as a more serious musician you'll find that your thumb is suddenly going off in bewildering directions. The thumb is just there to make sure that the rest of your fretting hand is comfortable.

Exercise: Try moving your hand around the guitar's neck, you don't need to be fretting anything, just make sure that your thumb is sitting comfortably no matter where you do it.

3. Don't Press Like A Bull, Nor Like A Feather- Putting the correct amount of pressure on a string is a bit of an art form. Put too little, and suddenly you aren't playing the right note, put too much, and suddenly you can't change from that sound. It could also cause injuries. To remedy this, try playing at higher BPM if you're pressing too hard, and lower BPM if you're pressing too softly.

Exercise: Pick a string, look up online how it's supposed to sound when played on a certain fret, and play it like that. Alternate pressure until you've got it just right.

4. Make Sure Your Fingers Are Close & Flexible- Okay so, while you should generally keep your fingers close to the fretboard, this isn't always the best idea. Sometimes, you'll

need to shift the angle of your hand to ensure your fingers are close enough. Depending on the size of your hands, you might need to adjust your angle to compensate quite often.

Exercise: Switch between different angles and check out how far your hand can reach on the fretboard all at once while remaining comfortable.

Finally, make sure your hand is comfortable. There's no theory in the world that will save you if your hand just doesn't feel good playing the instrument. While I've outlined some general tips here, that doesn't mean they're the be-all-end-all of hand positioning, so don't sweat it too much if you deviate from something I've said.
Let's take a look at some exercises you can do to make playing easier, shall we?

Exercises:

1. Try playing the aptly named "spider" exercise below, it's made to test the reach of your left hand.

2. The below exercise should help you a lot with synchronizing your left- and right-hand movements:

3. Number each fret, now start reading out pi. I'm serious, for every digit of pi, move to a chosen fret with one of your fingers. Try strumming with your right hand to make sure you're keeping up the right amount of pressure.

Chords

A chord is defined as any combination of three or more notes which are sounded together. They are the backbone of guitar music and are part of what sets guitar apart from the rest.

You've already seen most of the chords in this section, so you can go back and look them up if you need a refresher on how they look.

C, F, and D major chords are used in most popular music today and are easy to learn. Focus on them before on others. They are by far the easiest to learn, and you'll find that you can play hundreds of songs just by learning these three chords.

C major: This is probably the most common chord of all-time. It is made up of the C, E and G notes from the C major scale.

You should create a staircase-like shape using your second and third fingers. It could be hard to learn in the beginning because people tend to mute the high E string with their first finger so make sure to have proper finger positioning.

F major: This one has a very similar shape to the C major. But instead of leaving the G string open, you will need to hold your second finger on the second fret, and your third finger on the third fret of the D string. Moving between these two is the first chord switch you may learn since you keep the first finger is in the same position. You do not have to play the barre in the F major open chord.

A major: This entire chord is found on the second fret, which makes it a lot easier to play for new guitarists. Some people prefer to use fingers 1, 2, and 3 on the second fret of the D, G, and B strings but you can barre them with a single finger as well.

D major: This one uses a chord shape that is a bit different from the chords mentioned previously. It's easier to remember it as a triangle. Use your first two fingers to press on the second frets of the G and the high E string, then use your third finger to press on the third fret of the B string.

G major: You will have to twist your hand in a claw shape for this one. The most difficult part is to hit the high E string. Most people choose to use their middle finger to do this but during practice, you may end up using your pinkie as well. You will probably find it hard to switch to other chords from this one.

E major: This one is very similar to A major, and once you have mastered it, you will be able to learn barre chords. The E major also uses every string, so when the strings are not held, they are played completely open.
A minor: The A minor chord is the E major chord that you have moved up one string. You can play it as the A major, just move the note on the B string from second to the first fret. You will notice the sound gets much more melancholic.

D minor: The D minor chord is played similarly to the D major, but the note played on the E string is moved from the second to the first fret. Remember that the sixth and fifth strings are muted so do not strum them! This chord is good for playing arpeggios.

E minor: This one is almost the exact copy of the E major, the only difference is that it lacks the note on the G string.

B minor: this is the only chord mentioned here that is not played completely open. It is, however, a very common shape and serves as a good introduction to the barre chords. The B minor chord borrows a similar pattern to the F major chord, played on the second fret, but it's played a string higher. To practice it properly, try playing it by barring from the first to the first to the fifth string. Make sure to mute the low E string, because it might sound a bit unnatural if you play it along with the others.
You'll find in later chapters that there's a variety of chords out there, including barre, power, and other kinds of chords which make your guitar-playing a lot more enticing.

Exercises:

1. Start by playing the C, F, and D chords. Make sure you're comfortable switching between them. It won't be easy at first, but as long as you do it in order it should be relatively easy.

2. Start doing it out of order, start randomly switching from chord to chord. If you've got someone to help you, you could have them say the names of different chords as you play.

3. Now you can start going through the different chords out there, you'll find that the G, C, and D chords are the ones most often used in music today. Repeat exercises 1 and 3, but with all the chords in this chapter.

4. Knockin' On Heaven's Door by Bob Dylan is a great song to start with. Get some tabs and get rocking. This song only contains the G, C, and D chords, so it should be fairly easy for you to start playing it. Here are the notes:

KNOCKIN ' ON HEAVEN'S DOOR

Easy Solo Guitar
Bob Dylan

Music by Bob Dylan
Arranged for mySongBook by Jérémy Cauliez

1/3

52

5. Start improvising! You know quite a few chords now, so it's time to jam. Try figuring out why some chords are called major, while others are called minor. See which ones

sound good together, while this exercise will probably take the most time, it's also the most worthwhile.

Chord Transitioning

The last few exercises will have introduced you to switching between chords, or chord transitioning. It's one of the most important things when it comes to playing the guitar. It isn't easy to just start going from chord to chord, and it's only natural you'll get a bit confused over time, however, there are some ways by which you can get better at doing this.

1. Stick Your Fingers Close to The Fretboard- While this won't always be the best way to play a certain chord, as a beginner, all you need is a way that will work, not necessarily the best one. By sticking close to the fretboard you ensure that your fingers won't spontaneously fly off of it.

2. Chords Are Made from The Lowest String- When I was just starting out, I always built my chords from the highest string. I'm not sure why. In the C major chord, I always started putting my fingers on the 2nd string first, and only then the rest. The issue is that you're most likely going to be playing the bottom strings first, so build your chords from there. When playing the C major chord, for example, put your fingers on the 5th, then 4th, and only then 2nd string. While this doesn't seem like a lot of time, it really adds up over time.

3. Learn to Move in Order- Another thing I was horrible at as a beginner. You should always prioritize moving the finger that has to go the biggest distance first. This way, you'll make sure that you're getting the most time to move the rest.

4. Don't Tense Up- I bet I'm starting to sound like a parrot right about now, but making sure your left hand is relaxed is crucial to moving quickly. The guitar has been made in order to facilitate the natural movement of your hand. But if your hand is more akin to an industrial crane grabbing onto it, well, that's when you'll be running into issues.

Exercises:

1. Write down the chords on a tab, starting from the lowest string and going upward. Then play them, this will get you into the habit of building your chords the right way, something that had eluded me for a while.

2. Play slowly, make sure that you're always moving your fingers in the most optimal way. While as a beginner, the milliseconds you might save moving from the C chord to the G chord might seem insignificant, it adds up on a higher level.

3. Attach a stick, or another straight object at a distance from the fretboard at which your fingers have to stick close to it. Now start playing, you'll be surprised by how much smoother it is!

Chapter 6
Right Hand Techniques

Your dominant (usually right) hand is called the strumming hand, although this is a bit of a misnomer as while it does handle strumming, it's also tasked with picking and maintaining the balance of the guitar.

Strumming

Strumming is the process of playing the guitar in such a way that you hit a bunch of notes at the same time. It's the "natural" way to play the guitar you see in most TV shows, and also the way you've been playing chords so far.

You might be surprised to find it out, but strumming does have its own notation!

$$\sqcap \ = \ \textbf{Downstroke}$$
$$\lor \ = \ \textbf{Upstroke}$$
$$\times \ = \ \textbf{Mute}$$

By using these simple signs, we can create complex strumming patterns that you'll soon learn about. Learning to strum is extremely crucial to your playing as a guitarist. Being a guitarist and not knowing how to strum well is like being a pianist without any hands, sure, maybe you can hit a note, but you aren't using the instrument to its fullest potential.

Exercises:

1. Strum the following pattern:

1 & 2 & 3 & 4 &

Sure, it's all downstrokes, but while it seems easy, it won't be all that easy to keep up with it. Don't knock on these simple exercises as a beginner. This is what will eventually shape up to be a more complex exercise that you might even have trouble with.

2. Play the same pattern, but more dynamic. By this, I mean that you should experiment with sounds. Try getting slow, then going louder, then getting really loud. What you'll notice is that your tempo also changes. Make sure you get this under control before continuing onto the next exercise.

3. For the next exercise, strum the same pattern as before, just that every second stroke is an upstroke instead. Write this strumming pattern on a piece of paper. This will be important if you ever end up composing your own music.

4. Okay now, start muting every third stroke. I know it'll be hard to do at first, but you've got to learn it. To write this down, you write the muting symbol above the one for the stroke. To master muting is to master the audience. Remember, for as long as you aren't content just playing your guitar in your basement for all eternity, you're playing your audience before you're playing the guitar.

5. Write your own! Don't feel like you should always be constrained by someone else's strumming pattern. You need to experiment and get your own sense of style. Start writing out your own strumming patterns and play them.

Fingerpicking

Fingerpicking is a lot different from strumming the guitar. When you strum, you play a set of notes, while picking allows you to play each individually. In a way, it's closer to playing the piano than it is to strumming.

First, you'll want to train up your thumb:

Exercises:
1. Put your thumb onto the strings, and simply play the last three strings twice. That's it, you're just working your way up the three strings using just your thumb.
2. Now, start playing down the strings, again, do it twice each time. Make sure that your thumb is in front of the rest of your fingers, and that it's pointed towards the neck.
3. Start adding a small rhythm to it, keep in mind that your thumb needs to stay straight while you're doing this.

As with literally everything else in the universe, fingerpicking too has notation. The shorthand for each finger is:
I- Index Finger
M-Middle Finger
P- Thumb
A- Ring Finger

The pinky is very rarely used, and you won't be needing it as a beginner. Let's get into some simple patterns for you to pick, shall we?

Exercises:

1. Play this simple picking pattern:

4-5-6: P

3: I

2: M

1: A

I know going up and down the strings like this can be a bit annoying, but trust me, you'll be thanking your lucky stars for this exercise when you get to the more difficult ones.

2. Mix it up a little, you could play the following pattern:

4-6-5: P

3: I

2: M

1: A

You'll note that only one string has changed, however, it isn't as simple to play as the one before. This is because when it comes to picking, things aren't always as they seem.

Fundamentally, when you're learning how to fingerpick, there isn't a big secret to it. The more varied the patterns you do, the better you'll get. Unfortunately, it's one of those parts of playing the guitar that is essentially purely mechanical.

3. Start making your own fingerpicking pattern, the first step is to pick one that is 3-8 notes long. For now, just decide upon the notes.

4. Start it with the thumb, you'll want to assign only one note for the thumb for now, you get to choose this one, it'll be the starting note of your pattern.

5. Use a random number generator, that's the rest of your fingers. Yes, these can sometimes get a bit messy, but that's the point. Sometimes, fingerpicking will mean that you have to get into some very uncomfortable positions with your hand. Because of this, you'll want to ensure your fingers are ready for it.

With that being said, generally, you'll want your thumb to be tasked with the 1st three strings. The rest of your fingers should be assigned as follows:

Index finger- G string.
Middle finger- B string.
Ring finger- E string.

While it's allowed to have fun with this order, as a beginner, it's usually best to start off with something that already works.

6. Pick a song you've strummed before. Let's say Knockin' On Heaven's Door. Now, I want you to pick that song. It'll definitely be slower than strumming it, but it'll help you learn how to fingerpick much faster than a random exercise.

Chapter 7
Strength, Speed, and Dexterity

The three words you see in the title of this chapter aren't what you'd usually consider the hallmarks of a guitarist. They associate more with say, a boxer or an Olympic runner. Despite this, finger strength, speed, and dexterity are extremely important to a successful guitar career.

Sure, you can move some hearts playing slow blues music, but if you'd like to stay at the forefront of the industry, you've got to build that finger muscle!

The strength of your fingers is more important in your fretting hand than it is in your strumming hand. You need to be strong enough not only to press down on the string with the appropriate amount of strength but also to regulate it so it doesn't vary. Furthermore, you'll need to do this for hours on end if you want to be successful.

Speed and dexterity are similar. Everyone finds it mesmerizing to look at a great guitarist's hands while they play. They seem almost as if they're flashing in and out of existence. Unfortunately, these qualities don't emerge out of thin air, and there's a lot of practice to be had before you start playing like that.

Exercises: Let's begin with some simple physical hand exercises to get us started:

1. Crack your knuckles- if you're someone that gets air trapped in their knuckles, that can easily get in the way of your playing or even lead to injury. Despite popular belief, there's nothing medically bad about cracking your knuckles. Doing this before playing will make it a lot easier to relax your hands.

2. Stretch- I don't mean just stretching out the fingers of your hand, stretch out your whole body. You'll be sitting in the same spot, probably slightly hunched over, for a few hours. To avoid any injury, make sure that you're stretched, putting more focus on your hands.

3. Take your guitar, put your fingers on the first 4 frets of the first string. Now, what you'll want to do is start shifting each finger to the string underneath. Make sure that you're keeping your hand still while doing this.

These basic hand exercises are there to get you prepped for playing. It's important that you focus on which area you want to improve. You won't have much luck if you're trying to improve strength, speed, and dexterity at the same time.

There's a different set of exercises depending on what you're pursuing to enhance at the current moment.

Single Note Exercises

If the stuff so far was there to get you physically ready to play, this is here to improve your physicals as well as getting your mind ready for it. The reason why we do this kind of exercise is that a warmup shouldn't be difficult per se. Instead, it should be just challenging enough that you have to pay attention, but nothing beyond that.

A single-note exercise will have your fretting hand move one finger at a time. This'll help blood circulate around your fingers. This is the type of motion that lets you play the guitar.

We'll be taking a look at 2 different one-note exercises here, so get ready for them!

Exercises:

1. Okay so, this next exercise isn't exactly the pinnacle of musical craftsmanship, however, it will get the blood going through your fingers.

You play this for the pattern, rather than for the musical meaning. Basically, what you'll be doing is alternating your fretting hand's fingers, while picking the same notes over and over again. It's quite an easy exercise to pull off, but it's quite effective at building speed.

2. Underneath you'll find another exercise:

At first, it might seem similar to the first, but try playing it! This exercise is great for dexterity, as it demonstrates a diagonal pattern across the guitar's neck. It'll force your fretting hand to change positions, which is great for practice.

These exercises can only really get you so far. When it comes to practicing your dexterity, speed, and strength, nothing does it as well as an actual song, which is why our next 2 exercises will be focusing exactly on that:

Exercises:

1. Take a look at Zombies by The Cranberries

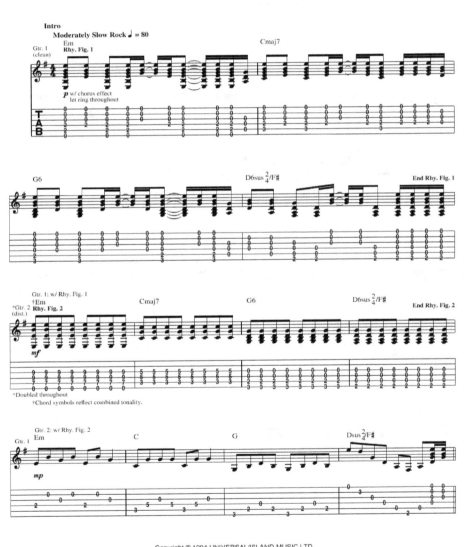

Zombie

Lyrics and Music by Dolores O Riordan

1146

It's quite likely this is the biggest composition you've played so far, however; it shouldn't be too difficult to get around. It involves only basic chords after all. Film yourself while playing this song, then compare and contrast to the original. Chances are, there are small nooks and crannies in the way you play the song. You'll want to iron these out, and you'll see that fixing these small mistakes actually carries with it large improvements.

2. Take a look at Dust In The Wind by Kansas:

Dust in the Wind

Words and Music by Kerry Livgren

This is a great song to practice fingerpicking with. While fingerpicking doesn't do wonders for your speed, it'll boost your strength and dexterity. Give it a treatment close to the one you gave the Cranberries. Since this song is a bit more difficult, it's alright to play it in a slower BPM, for as long as you play it correctly.

Chapter 8

Coordination is the Key!

When you play the guitar, everything you hear is produced by your right hand, which modifies everything your left-hand forms. When you are a rhythm guitarist, you provide a base for everyone else: the singer, the melodic instruments, and you also help the sounds of bass and drums sound sensible. You are essentially providing the whole musical experience.

A Refresher

Before learning how to play rhythms and practice your left and right hand, you need to learn tempo, time annotation, and rhythm annotation.

The tempo is the speed of which a pattern is being played. It is measured in beats per minute (BPM). For example, if we talk about a song being played at 150 BPM, that means 150 beats are being played each minute.

Beats are placed within bars, which are just sections of music that help us keep track of it. Any number of beats can be placed within a bar. They are separated with bar lines. A single bar line represents the end of a bar, a double represents the end of a passage in the musical piece. The double bar line with a thickened second line represents the end of the whole piece.

Time signatures show us how many beats are played within a bar, and what note they are. These are found at the beginning of each tab. The top number indicates how many beats are in a bar, and the bottom one which note is played. Common time signatures are 3/4, 4/4, 6/8, 12/8. 3/4 means that there are three beats in each bar and that the bars contain quarter notes. 4/4 means that the bars have four beats and that they contain quarter notes. The same logic applies to 6/8 and 12/8.

The definition of strumming is: dragging your guitar pick or your fingers across the strings. In the beginning, you should only drag the pick downward. This will play all the sound the left hand creates. You do this in ordinary, equal strokes, one per beat, all the while you follow the tempo (the musical rate). Subsequently, you create rhythm. A quarter-note rhythm to be exact, which is good for playing emotional, melancholic songs. This note takes up one beat only. It has a full head and a stem.

If you wish to get out of the pale rhythm of the quarter-note pattern of playing, you should try and play eighth notes. This means you will have to strum two times more frequently than in quarter-note patterns. In other words, you will have to play two strums per beat, contrary to what you might be used to, which is only one strum per beat. Just move your hands two times faster than you usually would. This is simple at slow and moderate tempos, but at fast tempos, you will have to alternate between upstrokes and downstrokes.

In playing eighth notes, you cannot only rely on slashes, but also slashes with stems and beams (quarter lines coming from the head of the note, and the thick horizontal lines that bind the stems, respectively). This is because quarter notes are attached to single stems, while eighth notes are attached to beams that bind them to other eighth notes. A lone eighth note has a flag instead of a beam. The note heads are not the same as ones depicting distinct pitches, but elongated and under an angle, and they indicate specific rhythmic values.

Upstrokes and Downstrokes

A downstroke is defined as the motion that moves the pick down, pulling on several strings while doing it. This is done quickly, even when the tempo is slow, so they are played almost at the same time. A chord is made when you play more than two notes while doing this.

An upstroke is shown by a sign V, and its definition is simple: an opposite of a downstroke. You start below the strings and drag the pick upwards, as opposed to a downstroke where you start above the strings and pull down. You might find this a bit odd as it is not the most natural way of playing, the reason being that you oppose the force of gravity. With enough practice, you will find it easy to perform both upstrokes and downstrokes, but this will, of course, take time. Upstrokes are used when you play the off beats when you play your eighth notes, between the beats of the quarter-notes.

The reason you should focus on playing them only in these instances is because there are not a lot of musical pieces where you use only upstrokes in any section. You can find many songs that are played only with downstrokes, but none with upstrokes. So, focus on playing them where they usually live - eighth notes, between the beats of the quarter-notes. As a beginner, don't think about hitting all the strings while doing an upstroke. This is usually unnecessary, as hitting the first three or four strings is more than enough. This is the case with the E chord, and you don't have to bother about thinking if you've hit all the strings or not. By the time you reach the third string, your hand will curl toward the center of the guitar naturally anyway.

Upstrokes are played most naturally as a counter-response to downstrokes. Try playing a song with a 4/4 time signature, where there are four beats in each measure, and each quarter-note is played per beat. Play it in an up-and-down hand motion, taking care that you put equal emphasis on each swing. At a slow tempo, you can even play it solely using downstrokes. This might have a negative side-effect if you are playing a melancholic song, this might make the sound more robust and aggressive than it's supposed to be. This might be a good thing if you are playing a rock song or a metal song though. You should try to play songs at fast tempos with all downstrokes, as adding upstrokes might sound unnatural and almost slow the tempo down. Decide to use only downstrokes or combine them with upstrokes based on the personal feel of the song, although you will find the alternating much easier when you play eighth notes.

Sixteenth notes are played at double speed from eighth notes, four per beat to be exact. This is why they are always played in alternating downstrokes and upstrokes, as doing only downstrokes would come across as very challenging and unnatural. Certain punk-rock and metal bands play their sixteenth notes this way, but this requires a lot of practice and a good technique, and also fits the songs as they are usually very aggressive. It doesn't fit your everyday pop or rock song though. If you want to practice sixteenth note strumming, you can do it on "Pinball Wizard" by Who. It begins with a common sixteenth-note figure, at a medium tempo progression. True syncopation (which is rhythms employing both dots and ties) stay out of the question until you perfect the basics. If you somehow bump into a rhythm notation that you find hard to understand because it's condensed, focus on memorizing the figures and ignore the notation. You need to be able to play properly, and notations are not essential for this.

Rhythmically playing the guitar has many more approaches than a few simple strums of chords.

Guitar players usually use the same technique as their piano-playing colleagues, who separate the left and the right hand to play bass notes and chords separately, respectively. If a guitarist splits the parts of the chords he does not use his hands separately but uses his right hand to play both. This is called a pick-strum pattern. By distinguishing the bass and the treble you add rhythmic diversity and introduce different shapes of the chords.

The simplest accompaniment pattern is known for its distinct name: boom-chick. The boom-chick pattern is efficient because you don't have to do all the notes of the chord at once. The bass note would usually be played on a boom, and all other notes of the chord on the chick — but you get some acoustic credit for playing this twice.

A crucial musical device you can use after you separate the bass from the chord is the mobile bass line. Notable songs with mobile bass lines include "Southern Man" by Neil Young, Led Zeppelin's "Babe, I'm Gonna Leave You", "Friend of the Devil" by the Grateful Dead and "Mr. Bojangles" by the Nitty Gritty Dirt Band. A mobile bass line can apply the boom-chick pattern. It applies left-hand usage in chord playing, weirdly.

Syncopation

When you have mastered different combinations of the quarter, eighth and sixteenth notes, you can add a bit of a twist by using syncopation. The definition of this is to disrupt how the notes are expected to sound. This is especially applicable to rock 'n' roll right-hand rhythm playing, and you do it by striking different parts of beats by tottering your strums and mixing downstrokes and upstrokes. This makes your rhythmic strumming take a much more interesting and unexpected pattern.

Syncopation is annotated using dots and ties.

When a dot is bound to a note, it increases the note's rhythmic value by 1.5 times. For example, if you attach it to a half note, it makes it three beats long, instead of two. In syncopation, you connect two notes of the same pitch with a curvy line, and this is a tie. This means that you only sound the first note, but its rhythmic value will be equal to the combined rhythmic values of the two connected notes. To practice this try playing two progressions, one using eighth notes and one using sixteenth notes, then apply frequent rock music syncopations to them. In the beginning, try ones at 4/4 rhythm in moderate tempos. These are easy and good for beginners. Always remember that the normal flow of upstrokes and downstrokes is disrupted in syncopation, so make sure to always follow the upstroke and downstroke indications because otherwise, you will find it hard to play the pattern.

Muting

Carefully listen to the rhythm guitar in rock music, you will hear that the strummed pattern are not singular acoustic bodies, but that small stops occur between the strums. These exist to prevent chord strums from "leaking" into one another, thus creating a chaotic, meaningless sound. These small stops help you control the sound and keep it meaningful. When you are trying to create these acoustic pauses, you need to stop the strings from ringing for a short amount of time. These have to be extremely short though. Imagine if you coordinated your right hand's gas pedal with your left hand's brake pedal.

This is a good way of thinking about it and helps you better understand this technique.

To do this with your left hand, you will need to relax your fingers which you use for fretting, to alleviate the pressure on the fretted strings. These will then stop vibrating immediately, muting the sound in the process. If you wish to create a pleasant thunk sound you can still strum the immobilized strings, hitting all of them, in the same strumming pattern. By using this aghast technique, combined with all the ringing notes, you can create a sound that is pleasantly robust, moving and powerful. This is ideal for rock music. Going a step further, you can completely relax your left hand, muting all the strings by doing so, and continue to play your normal pattern of upstrokes and downstrokes. This relaxing of the left hand is annotated in musical writing with the symbol X on the note head.

A technique of muting your right hand also exists, and it includes using the bottom of your right-hand palm. This technique is often called chugging in the guitarist community. You do this by putting the bottom of your right hand on the strings and applying pressure to them. Take care not to go too far with your hand as you will completely immobilize the strings. Apply just enough pressure so that the strings become dampened - they are still ringing but not as intensively as before.

This, however, produces a different effect from left-hand muting. When you mute your right hand, you will still hear the fretted string, but in a tranquilized way. This is because muting your right hand has a different purpose to muting your left hand. When you mute your left hand, you want to stop the sound entirely. When you use right-hand muting, your goal is to prevent the string from ringing uncontrollably. Just as left-hand muting, right-hand muting prevents the tone from undergoing unwanted ring-outs, and also gives the notes a distinct, unclear foggy sound, which is good for dramatic effect and building up tension. These are way easier to play if you strike only one or two strings because the right hand is partially immobilized while applying pressure on the strings near the bridge. Keep the hand in place as long as you play the strum. If a palm mute (another name for the right-hand muting technique) manages to draw attention away from the string strike, then you employ an accent, to draw the attention back to the string strike. This one is easy to perform, just hit the strings harder than you do usually, or lift the right hand from the string so you allow the strings to ring freely. This allows the strum you are putting an accent on to stand out and sound over other strums. Accents are annotated with the symbol > written above or under the note head.

Most of what you cover as a beginner is a constant right-hand movement to produce whatever the immobile left hand manages to form. Once you begin to move your left hand alongside your right, you will discover a completely new way of approaching guitar playing - right-hand production of rhythm accompanied by left-hand movement. By setting your left hand free, you are making the first step towards playing the lead guitar and the single note riffs. Classic left-hand patterns fit inside the straight eighth-note setting. In this example, the notes are changing from the fifth degree of every chord immediately to the sixth degree. For example, in an A chord, the E moves to F#; in a D chord the A moves to B, and in an E chord the B moves to C#. This pattern does not have a standardized name and you will encounter different synonyms as you learn more. It is one of the more prominent patterns in songs of jazz, blues and rock genre. This pattern fits over any I-IV-V progression, but try playing it in the key of A, it's the easiest one.

Chapter 9

Mastering Your Guitar Arpeggio

Arpeggios are notes of a chord that are played individually, rather than strummed together. This is why they are often referred to as broken chords.

Before you start playing arpeggios, it is important to distinguish between them and scales. Scales are a series of notes played to fit within a specific key signature, while arpeggios are sets of notes played within a single chord. They both are linear, in other words, notes are played one at a time, but they differ in the fact that notes can go outside specific chords, while arpeggios are restricted to them. For example, the G major scale would be G, A, B, C, D, E, F#, while the G major arpeggio is restricted to G, B, D.

When you used arpeggios, you are creating a fast, flowing sound. They add to speed in your playing and are also good for improvisations. Because they have all of the notes of their chords, you can link them to the chord structure that is played beneath you if you are doing a solo. They also sound good over their matching chords in a progression, and this allows you to have a safe base if you are a beginner at improvising on the guitar.

Although they add to the speed of your playing, you should learn to play arpeggios slowly. Every note needs to be distinct from other notes. Mute each note immediately after picking it by lifting the fretting finger. This might be boring at the beginning but if you do not perfect this the notes might start "leaking" into one another and produce a sound similar to a strummed chord. This can become a bad habit that will take much time to correct.

If you are new to arpeggios, you should always start and end them on the note upon which the chord is built – the root note. Start with the lowest-pitched root note, proceed up as far as possible, then back down as low as you can, and then return to the root note.

Various shapes exist in playing arpeggios. Generally, there are five shapes for each of the arpeggios. The exception is the diminished seventh, which only has one shape. When you learn different arpeggios, learn them on the different positions of the neck of the guitar so you don't have to concentrate on which frets you should put your fingers in. This way you will be free to think about learning the shape of the arpeggio itself. To learn them properly you should learn them one at a time. You will have to learn all the five shapes of each, but it's better to play one or two of them properly rather than all of them badly. Always practice moving from one shape to another in both ways.

Major Arpeggios

Major Arpeggio 1: To play this arpeggio pattern you will have to use your first finger of your left hand to play the first note which is found on the fifth position on the guitar neck. Major arpeggio 1 includes two out-of-position notes (these do not fall under the four-fret span defined by the position, so they require you to stretch your first or fourth finger to play). They are found on the sixth and first strings. You will have to stretch your fourth finger up (near the bridge) to play the note found one fret higher from the one you would normally play. This is a good physical exercise because it includes, and subsequently expands, the in-between fingers. To loosen your left hand, play the first two notes back and forth several times before trying to play the whole pattern. Practice the pattern as many times as you need to start feeling comfortable with it.

Major arpeggio 2: This pattern does not include any out-of-position notes and starts with your fourth finger on the sixth string. This pattern does not require you to stretch your fingers so you may focus on other skills. For instance, you can flatten out your first finger to play consecutive notes that occur at the same fret, such as the ones on the forth, third, and second strings (occurring on the fifth fret in this case). Imagine your first finger to be a mini barre (a partial barre covering two or three strings). This technique helps you create smooth and connected legato sounds between the notes. Practice this pattern until you can successfully play it several times in a row, including the mini-bare finger altering's.

Previous major patterns have a range of two or more octaves, but major arpeggio 3,4, and 5 have a range that spans less than two octaves. This means your exercises will get shorter as there are fewer notes to play, but you will find it easier to memorize these.

Major arpeggio 3: Unlike the previous patterns which begin on the sixth string, major arpeggio 3 begins on the fifth. You start it with your first finger and it also includes an out-of-position note on the fifth string. To reach the out-of-position note, you must stretch up (near the bridge) with your fourth finger, because it's found one fret above (higher on the neck) where the finger would naturally fall. Practice the pattern until you get the stretch feeling comfortable. 3 also provides an opportunity to try using alternate fingerings to make the arpeggios easier to play in legato passages. Attempt to form a mini barre using your third finger to play any note combinations that consecutively fall on the fourth, third, and second strings. In an exercise, you can try and create a legato sound in the 8th-position F major, by using a third-finger mini-barre at the tenth fret for the strings named above. By doing so you will make playing the sixteenth notes easier.

Major arpeggio 4: You should practice this pattern very slowly, don't worry about the rhythm. Here it is important to play all the notes equally well, and you can practice the

75

rhythm once you have accomplished this. In an exercise try playing the third position E major. Try playing it in both staccato and legato. The former means playing each note with a fingertip and immediately letting go, while in the latter you want to hold the left hand down as a chord and let the notes ring out when you can. This is possible because you can hold the first five notes as a chord.

Major arpeggio 5: This is a four-string pattern which has it's the lowest note on the fourth string. Starting with the first finger, it includes an out-of-position note on the fourth string. As it is the case with the major 3, you will have to stretch your fourth finger up (near the bridge), because this note occurs one fret above where the finger would naturally fall. Mind that, while including the starting finger next to the first note while playing, you will also include the fingering for the out-of-position note (on the fourth string). To get back into the pattern, you will have to move your finger back to the third string. To make a smooth move from the fourth string to the third string, you need to prioritize practicing this move before you focus on rhythmic exercises.

Minor Arpeggios

Minor arpeggio 1: Try playing the A minor arpeggio on the fifth position on the neck of the guitar. Play the first note by using the first finger of your left hand.

This arpeggio does not include any out-of-position notes (the ones that fall outside of the four-fret span defined by the position), you do not need to stretch your first and fourth finger. This makes this pattern ideal for getting familiar with minor arpeggios. At fast tempos, you can try using your finger as a mini barre to play consecutive strings at the same fret. Try playing this in the key of F minor at first position. However, closely monitor your rhythm here as people tend to rush up and drag on their way down the arpeggio. The best way to practice this is with the help of a metronome.

Minor arpeggio 2: This pattern has seven notes, and the fourth finger covers four of them, so during this exercise concentrate on your fourth finger and building up its strength. Keep your fingers curved at all times by not letting the knuckles flatten! Try practicing minor arpeggio 2 in 2nd-position A minor. To accomplish a legato effect, try using the fourth finger as a mini barre over the three strings on the top. To make this easier, try putting the third finger over the fourth and pushing down with both of them.

As with the major arpeggios, the first two patterns have a range of more than two octaves, while the last three have a range smaller than that. This, of course, makes the exercises shorter and easier to memorize.

Minor arpeggio 3: Try playing this in the key of D minor. Play all the notes slowly so they are distinct from one another and clear. After you have accomplished this, build up the speed to prepare for the rhythmic exercises. Then try playing it in third position C minor. For a legato, use a third finger mini barre across the third and fourth string, and for staccato simply play the string separately also using the third finger.

Minor arpeggio 4: As with most patterns make sure to practice playing the notes separately and clearly before you start practicing the rhythmic side. Now try playing the #4 minor pattern in third position E minor. Do this by playing the second string with your second finger. This helps you keep in position. To reach the first first-string note, stretch the finger down near the nut. To eliminate the stretch between the second and first strings, substitute the third finger with the second finger on the second string.

Minor arpeggio 5: Try playing this in a key of G minor. Play the pattern slowly so your fingers get used to playing the notes which fall on the different strings and frets. Once you have accommodated to this, speed up so you can move on to rhythmic exercises. When you feel comfortable with the pattern, give the exercise in the seventh position of A minor a try. If you wish to avoid using the fourth finger, you can try using the following technique: starting with the second note, use fingers 3-2-3-1 (and not 4-3-4-2) and make sure to play all the notes staccato, so you can distinctly hear them.

Seventh Arpeggios

Major seventh chord arpeggio 1: This pattern includes three out-of-position notes — on the sixth, second, and first strings. You need to stretch up your fourth finger (near the bridge) to reach these notes, as they are found one fret above from where the finger usually falls. Whatever seventh chords you encounter while playing, the so-called tonic major seventh chord will be one of them (the exception being a major seventh chord in blues, which normally employs all dominant seventh chords). This is why it is important to master major seventh chord arpeggios, as they outline all the notes of the seventh chord in major.

Major seventh chord arpeggio 2: Try playing this pattern in the key of C. The middle part can be hard to master, so at first try to play just the notes on the fourth, third, and second strings in an ascending loop that goes, by fingers, as follows: 1-4-1-1-4. Move back down again. Practice this loop in isolation at least four times before running the entire pattern up and down. For a more legato sound, flatten your first finger to play the consecutive notes of the third and second strings. Practice the loop in isolation before you try playing the whole pattern in both ways.

Major seventh chord arpeggio 3: In comparison to previous patterns, this one has a span lesser than two octaves, which makes it easier to memorize and master. Feel free to repeat the notes if you need to do so to fulfill the idea of the arpeggio, however, make sure to think creatively so you don't end up with just a simplified, longer pattern. Try playing it in the key of D. You might find it hard in the beginning as it has two out-of-position notes and a possible mini barre between the third and second strings. You do not have to isolate the passages as the pattern is very short, you just have to play the complete pattern until you can overcome the challenging aspects and play them as easily as the other ones. Note that this means you might have to practice it many more times than any other pattern.

Minor seventh arpeggio 1: Try playing this sequence in A minor. There is only one spot where you can consider replacing a mini barre for the same finger hop across the two strings, and that is between the third and second strings. To see which technique you find most comfortable, play both the same number of times so deduce which one suits you better. A good exercise is in the third position in key G minor. A good way to practice legato is to barre all six strings with your first finger and keeping it in place. Then gradually add the fourth and third fingers when appropriate.

Minor seventh chord arpeggio 2: This pattern is a lot harder to play then all the previous ones, as it relies heavily on your fourth finger. To make it a bit easier, flatten your fourth finger to play the consecutive notes of the third and second string. It also helps with creating a legato between the notes.

Minor seventh chord arpeggio 3: This pattern has a range of lesser than two octaves, but as with the major seventh chord 3, you can fill it in by double-striking notes, changing directions, etc. This pattern has no out-of-position notes, and you will not have to employ any alternate fingerings. Alternate between the legato and staccato in this pattern until you can play them both equally well.

Exercises:

1. Let's take a look at an arpeggio exercise. You'll want to look at arpeggios as simply stacks of third intervals. So, let's say we take the A minor scale, which is A B C D E F G. The A minor arpeggio simply skips the B and D notes, making it A C E. You can easily do this ad nauseam no matter how many times you wanted.

When playing the following exercise, I want you to do more than just imprint what's on the tab into your head. I want you to learn every note you're playing. You should visualize them going up and down in relation to the A minor scale.

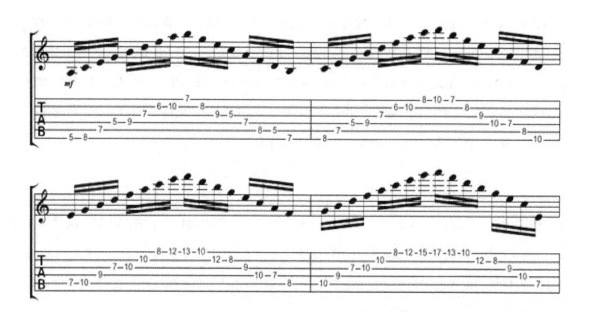

2. Play the B minor scale. While doing this, start skipping every second note. This'll simulate the way arpeggios are formed, and you'll come out of it with a better understanding of what arpeggios are.

3. Take the arpeggios you've learned so far and find out which scales they belong to! There's a reason we haven't been naming them for you. Remember the process through which an arpeggio is made and get on with it!

Chapter 10
Guitar Playing Tips

For the final chapter of this book, you can rest a little. Good job on getting this far! You've conquered over 70 exercises to get here. By doing that, you've shown a lot of promise as a future guitar player.

With that in mind, I would love to leave you off with some tips on how to expand your skills and work on your career:

1. Market Yourself- A lot of aspiring guitarists make this mistake; they think that their playing will speak for themselves. Well, unless you play like Buckethead, that's quite unlikely. If you want to be serious about the guitar, you'll need some marketing skills. In reality, being a musician is almost as much about being a good marketer as it is being a good musician. Open a YouTube channel, and try to maintain an active social media presence. You want prospective clients or bands to see the best side of you possible.

Let's take an example. Some rich guy wants to hire you to play at his yacht bar for a party. In which scenario are you more likely to get this job, the one where the first thing that pops up is your carefully curated YouTube channel and Instagram account with 50k followers...Or if what he found was a shoddily-filmed video off a phone of your concert 5 years ago?

2. Use A Metronome- This really can't be stressed enough. You might think you're always perfectly on tempo, but you're not. You had an excuse back when metronomes were 50-60 USD each, today you can just download an app on your phone. Using a metronome

will not only ensure you stay on tempo but will also help you in establishing a better sense of rhythm.

3. Don't Try to Choke Your Guitar- The "death grip" is a fairly common thing for beginner guitarists to do. They just grip the guitar with as much strength as they've got and pray everything works out.

Well, while that might work for agent 007 when choking someone out, it doesn't bode quite as well for playing a musical instrument. All you're doing is making the sound worse and making it harder on yourself to actually play since you're holding onto it too hard to be flexible.

Remember that your hands are meant to be nimble and dexterous while playing, rather than rigid and strong. Using the barest minimum of strength for holding down the fret firmly is the hallmark of a good guitarist.

4. Make Sure to Practice Standing Too- If most of your practice sessions are held sitting down, don't worry about it. Pretty much every guitarist is like that. However, you'll still need to learn how to play standing up. Playing standing up is almost a whole different beast compared to playing sitting down. The audience loves it when you stand up, so make sure you practice standing up at least a bit every day.

5. Keep Your Guitar in Tune- Tune your guitar before every practice session. No exceptions. Keeping your guitar in tune is crucial to being able to tell your errors apart from the parts you played correctly. Plus, it makes your guitar sound a lot better. Even if you don't have access to a tuner at hand, just tune the guitar to itself, you can use the guide in chapter 1 for that.

6. You Aren't in Need for Speed- While it might work for actors on the big screen, or flamenco performers, there really isn't a need to do a night core version of Wonderwall for no reason.

Guitar playing isn't about speed, it's about accuracy. Instead of playing quickly but sloppily, it's much better to play slowly but accurately. Make sure you aren't making any mistakes playing a song slowly before you start speeding up. I know it's fun to just step on the gas and check out how quickly you can rock out, but it doesn't serve a point past testing how fast your hands can go.

7. Jam, A Lot- While the exercises presented in this book are great and all, they alone can't make you a good guitarist. They'll instill in you the fundamentals, but then it'll be up to you to develop your own style. This is where jamming comes in. Jamming refers to either playing freestyle by yourself or doing so with another musician.

Personally, I find that jamming by myself is the best road to improvement. It lets you gauge where you're at, as well as pushing your creativity further and further. It's a different experience to play when you don't have notes or tabs to stare at in front of you.

Jamming with another musician is great if you're planning to get into a band, or you're one of those people that gains inspiration from playing with others. The great thing about doing this is it'll teach you how to build a supporting melody, instead of just a leading one.

8. Actually Use the Correct Fingering- If I had a dime for every student that went home, then came back to their lesson fingering a chord completely wrongly...well, let's just say I wouldn't work again. Fingerings have been kept up for hundreds of years for a reason. Chances are, if all the experts think that the best way to play certain notes and chords is one way, then that probably is the best way to do so.

Sure, sometimes you'll find a way to play them easier...until you have to switch to something. When there's an obvious better fingering, it's usually because that "better" fingering basically disables you from switching properly. So, at least while you're a beginner, don't mess with the fingerings...please.

9. Don't Be Afraid to Use Online Resources- Back in my day, we didn't have the internet. At least not to the extent that you have it now, use it. There's an abundance of YouTube tutorials out there for anything that isn't clear to you. There are hundreds of eBooks at your fingertips, so don't be afraid to look something up if you aren't sure about it.

The internet is also a goldmine for finding various different tabs and notes for songs. Seriously, if you can name a song, you can probably find its tabs online.

10. Take Breaks- This may seem quite strange. After all, how could practicing less end up working better? Well, by practicing past a certain point, you're just burning out. When you're done after a very long practice session, you'll probably feel very drained. To avoid this, you can take a break after every 15-30 minutes and take 5 minutes to just unwind, stretch, and relax your muscles.

11. Take Care of Your Hands- Your hands are the real instrument when you're playing the guitar. Don't let all of the nails of your strumming hand get long, they'll get in the way. Similarly, make sure to always trim the nails of your fretting hand, as having nails can distort the sound.

12. Move A Little Bit Each Day- It doesn't matter what it is, learn something new. It's more important to get into the habit of learning, than the things you actually learn. Even if you only pick up one small thing every day, within a year that's 365 things you've learned about the guitar. Wait for 3 years, and you're already over 1000 things. Plus, if you make it a habit, you're unlikely to ever stop on that road.

13. Learn Other Instrument's Solos- I was very tempted to use the word "steal" here but reading the solos of other instruments can be quite useful for guitar practice. You see, many guitar pieces suffer from being same-y. When you feel like you've gotten into a rut, or that everything you play sounds the same, bust out some piano notes from a band you've never heard of and start shredding on that guitar!

14. Learn Certain Musical Parts by Heart- Sure, playing off of notes is impressive to other guitarists, but it isn't going to do much to excite people at a party. Learning to play some easier solos can be a great boost to your self-esteem and it'll make you look great in front of your friends! Besides this, it also helps you improve your style and delivery. Basically, learning your favorite guitarist's solos will make you a much better showman.

15. When Things Are Too Easy, Limit Yourself- Sometimes there simply aren't enough easily available exercises for your skill level. At this time, you can take an easier piece, and add a restriction for it. For example, you're only able to play notes after the 8th fret. Or maybe you have to use legato for the whole song? The most important thing is that you're challenging yourself and experimenting with different sounds.

16. Practice in Front of a Mirror- Practicing in front of a mirror can give you a great insight into how you look when you are performing. While in an ideal world, this wouldn't matter, our world isn't like that. Your guitar playing is just as relevant as your showmanship is, so make sure you aren't giving a boring show. Plus, playing in front of a mirror will often make you aware of mistakes that you wouldn't otherwise be aware of.

17. Make Sure You Truly Enjoy It- I can drone on about this kind of practice and that kind of practice. I can give you the best exercises in the world and offer the best of tips. But if you aren't enjoying what you're doing, what's the point of it? Fundamentally, the guitar is there to be played if you love it. Sure, sometimes you might feel a small amount of dislike, or even hatred towards the instrument, but it's important to keep in mind that your

enjoyment of the guitar is vital to how well you play it. Playing frustrated doesn't help anything. If you're feeling down, take a rest, and pick your guitar back up when you're feeling better!

Finally, let's go over some exercises you can do no matter the situation:

Exercises:

1. Read your favorite songs out slowly. - I'm not saying you need to play them. Just read them out slowly strumming/picking at your guitar. Gaining familiarity with more complex pieces of music is a lot more useful than you might think. Later on, when you encounter things that you've just passed through before, they'll come a lot easier to you.

2. Practice right-hand strumming- Sometimes, it can be a good idea to just mute all the notes with your left hand and check what kind of rhythm you can make with just your strumming hand. The complexity of this rhythm is a good portion of what separates a mediocre guitarist from a good one.

3. Add your own twist to songs- Playing already written songs is one thing, jamming is another. In the middle of these two is taking a popular song and adding a new twist to it. Maybe you accentuate different notes? Maybe you add a new chord here and there? In any case, the important thing is you're adding to it, and learning how to improvise a performance doing so.

4. Take a few chords and do them as fast as possible- While this goes slightly against some of the tips above, what you should do is just take a bunch of chords and see how fast you can switch between them. Take care to stop every time you make a mistake. You could even challenge yourself to see how quickly you could run all the chords you know.

Conclusion

This book was made to accompany any beginner guitarist on their way to become an intermediate, or even professional one. I hope the exercises in this book have helped you accomplish that.

Shall we take a look at what we've learned so far?

- You learned about the origins of the guitar, how the first guitar was made, as well as the guitar's journey to becoming the instrument we all know and love today.
- We've covered the difference between acoustic and electric guitars. Unfortunately, we couldn't settle the debate once and for all, but I hope I helped you make your selection.
- I described the inner workings of the guitar, as well as how the various kinds of guitar make their unique sounds.
- You've learned every form of guitar notation under the sun. We started with simple chord diagrams and rhythm slashes but moved onto tabs and sheet music quickly.
- We went over how to maintain your body while you play. I told you what the necessary stretching and posture was in order to maintain health. We also went over some exercises that would help ease the burden playing puts on your body.
- We discussed the Pareto, AKA 20/80 principle, and how it could apply to your guitar playing.
- You learned about Parkinson's law, and with it, how to time your practicing sessions better than before.
- We looked at the importance of habit in not only learning the guitar, but also becoming a professional.
- I showed you some excellent fretting hand exercises, and we also went over how to improve your fretting abilities.

- Chords are no longer an unfamiliar, but begrudgingly accepted term. Now you're aware of many different chords and can play them proficiently.

- Arpeggios got a similar treatment to chords, where you learned not only to identify and play them, but also how to create arpeggios out of every scale.

- We went through the crucial strumming-hand techniques you needed to know in order to improve. We paid special attention to fingerpicking, as it's one of the more difficult guitar techniques.

- You learned about the importance of strength, speed, and dexterity in guitar playing. I also showed you some useful exercises on that front.

You've learned all of this and more in under 80 exercises! That has to be impressive, right?

It very much is, and I'd like to leave you off with the words of a famous guitarist:

"Sometimes you want to give up the guitar, you'll hate the guitar. But if you stick with it, you're gonna be rewarded."

-Jimi Hendrix

References

Bradshaw, S. (2016, May 20). How to Play Arpeggios on Guitar. Retrieved from https://www.cyberfret.com/guitar-arpeggios/arpeggios-for-guitar-primer/.

Falconer, J. (2017, November 14). How to Use Parkinson's Law to Your Advantage. Retrieved from https://www.lifehack.org/articles/featured/how-to-use-parkinsons-law-to-your-advantage.html.

Phillips, M., & Chappell, J. (2016). *Guitar for dummies*. Hoboken, NJ: John Wiley & Sons.

Reh, F. J. (2019, October 23). The Many Uses of Pareto Principle or the 80/20 Rule. Retrieved from https://www.thebalancecareers.com/pareto-s-principle-the-80-20-rule-2275148.

ULTIMATE GUITAR TABS - 1,100,000 songs catalog with free Chords, Guitar Tabs, Bass Tabs, Ukulele Chords and Guitar Pro Tabs! (n.d.). Retrieved from https://www.ultimate-guitar.com/.